PERSO
SIMPLIFIED

An easy to follow guide to personal development for beginners. Identify and break negative patterns. Become a better version of yourself. Guaranteed.

First Edition, 2017
www.alifewellcreated.com
Copyright © 2017 Kshitij Prasai (Coach KP).
All Rights Reserved

GRATITUDE

I am grateful for *all* that I have experienced in my life. It has made me who I am today. It hasn't always been easy, but it has been worth it.

First and foremost, I would like to thank Lord Shiva for protecting me from the perils of life. Without his guidance, this would have been a very short existence.

The list of who and what I should be grateful for is gigantic, I am sure it will not fit on a page, but I shall attempt to include as many names possible, starting with my mother Niraja Prasai for bearing me in her belly for nine months. There is no gift in the world greater than that. My Father Lakshmi Prasad Prasai. My Sister Dikshya Prasai and her husband Shail Neupane. My Late Grandmother Divyarupa Prasai. My Late Grandfather Jaya Prasad Prasai (Jiju) Prasai. My Grandfather Mahendra Dubadi. My Grandmother Padma Dubadi. My Ancestors above them. Ghattekulo, Kathmandu, Nepal. Anil & Parbati Sharma. Anish Sharma. Prerita Sharma. Bashudev Poudyal. Dr. Krishna Shrestha. Dirgha Raj Prasai. Prahlad Prasai. Dhiraj & Pranita Prasai. Dr. Phadindra Niraula & Nirmala Niraula. Prajwal Niraula. Amanda Williams. Alex & Melody Williams, Granny and everyone at the Holler in Artie, WV. Peggy Sue Brown. Pritaz Karki. Kreepa Aryal. Rojeen Adhikari. Subash Nepal. Saroj Aryal. Prakash Pandey. Anthony Robbins. Earl Nightingale. Les Brown. Suresh Yadav. Rupesh Yadav. Ranganathan Siriviaram. Kevin Powers. Brian Peter Carr. Binod & Pramila Adhikari. Dr. Sixin Quan. Prasun Vyas. Kunal Mehta.

Dinkins Drusior. Jesse Silverman. Frank Caloroso. Bhoj Bahadur Shah. Ralph Smart Infinitewaters. Kartika Nair Synchroshakti. Louise Hay. Dr. Brené Brown. Evan Twersky. Arjun Thapa Magar. Napoleon Hill. Finding Pedro. /r/selfimprovement. Melodie Beatie. Lexington, MA CODA. Benito. Giuseppe Di Pietro. Eliot Hulse. Teal Swan. LEAAP@Liberty. Mexico. The United States of America.

FOREWORD

Dear Continuous Learners,

I have a tremendous amount of love for the people that are willing to learn and use what they have learned to change their lives as well as the lives of others.

Despite the brevity and the simplicity of this book, the message is powerful. By reading the book and doing the work that I recommend, you will be well on your way to becoming the best version of yourself. I guarantee.

I believe that the material in this book is priceless. However, I priced it as low as I could without cutting a loss because I wanted to bring Personal Development to the public, without complicated concepts, intimidating language, and arcane rituals. The concepts I discuss here are tried and true. I have personally used them to enhance my life, and I want the same for you.

There are many exercises in the book that you will have to complete in order to fully reap the benefits of this book. Learning the concepts and doing the work will ensure your lasting success.

You are welcome to take away as little or as much as you can from this book. However, the hardest working farmers generally reap the biggest harvests. Keep that in mind while reading and concentrate on getting as much as you can out of these pages.

Before you embark on this wonderful journey, I would like to thank you for purchasing this book. I sincerely hope that one day you look back on the first time you saw it and think to yourself that it was the beginning of a life well created.

Good Luck!
Coach KP

Before You Begin

There is a lot of information in this book. I recommend reading it all at least once before you decide if it is right for you.

I make references to working with any resistance that comes up throughout the rest of the book. However, if you absolutely cannot make sense of a topic after a few reads, I recommend not to linger on it for too long, and to move on to the next. You can come back to it later.

This is a habit I recommend you carry over to your life as well. A lot of intelligent minds waste a tremendous amount of time pondering over what does not resonate with them at that moment in life. This is a strategy that will result in disappointment and lost time.

We must understand that living in a world full of stimuli, most of the stimulus we experience will not be of any use to us. It is equally as important to train ourselves not to pay attention to such stimuli as it is to learn what to pay attention to.

Let your journey to Personal Development begin.

About the Guarantee:

If after reading this book and doing the exercises you conclude that you derived no value from it, I will personally send you a refund of the exact amount you paid for the book, within a year of the purchase, no questions asked. Get my contact information from my publisher, or look me up on the internet.

This is the Coach's Promise to you.

How to Read This Book

I have spent hours learning and teaching about each one of the topics in the book. I recommend going over the material slowly, understanding and internalizing each lecture, then moving on to the next only after completely digesting the previous one.

I strongly suggest maintaining a journaling habit while reading this book. Also essential is a routine where you come back to the book at designated times without fail. I recommend contemplating what you read here often, during your day, until the concepts are crystal clear.

Once you complete the book, a good idea would be to revisit the lectures and evaluate how much it has helped you make a change.

Personal Development is a simple concept to learn, but it is not an easy one to implement. The progress you make will be indicative of the effort you put in while reading this book.

A few words of caution: If a topic is new or is presented in an unfamiliar style, the natural tendency is to reject it. I recommend that you do not skip over any section, no matter how you perceive it to be, at least at first. The material is presented to you with tremendous love, so please participate in all the quizzes and be deliberate about finishing the exercises. Answers to all the quizzes can be found within the book.

This book will work miracles if you work it, so work it. You're worth it!

Contents

SECTION I

In this section, I debunk the myths surrounding
Personal Development, (also referred to as PD)
and shed light on what the concept means.

Why do people resist the phrase "Personal Development"

The majority of people are not introspective. This is a fact of life. This does not mean they are bad people. What this simply means is that most people are happy with the status quo.

It takes significant time and courage to inventory our strengths and weaknesses and to affirm that there are areas in our lives that may not be up to the standards we have set for ourselves to live up to. Most people are simply too busy dealing with life to have time to think about this.

The idea of engaging in Personal Development/Self-Help to some people also means that there is something very wrong in their lives that needs to be fixed. People detest this idea because it makes them feel like a failure.

Many times, people do not understand that there may be areas in their lives that need work unless they go through an adverse life situation.

Sometimes, Personal Development is advertised as a cure-all, which also turns people off. Other times, people do not have adequate information about Personal Development and end up thinking that it is only the privilege of the wealthy and the powerful.

Whatever the case may be, one does not have to have serious character flaws to want to develop as a person!

What Personal Development is not

Personal Development is not a quick fix. It is also not an end to all problems. It is a misconception that Personal Development is a set of tools that will bring you instant results. It won't. At least, not in the beginning.

Personal Development will not necessarily change your circumstances. Neither is it something you set and forget.

So, what is Personal Development?

Personal Development, in its simplest form, is any experience that enables them to receive more joy, peace, health, success, and prosperity in life.

PD is directly related to finding and working towards fulfilling one's life purpose. PD is a continuous process of inheriting qualities that transform the person into a better human being.

Notice I wrote "better." There is always room to grow, no matter how great your growth has already been.

It is certain that anything that stops growing starts to experience death and eventually decays.

As a person develops more positivity, joy, acceptance of and gratitude towards others, they gain qualities like self-respect, confidence, a sense of responsibility, and an absence of approval seeking behavior.

PD hinges largely on your desire to change your life. Although it is not a quick fix, once you get on this journey, due to the energy you start to attract and the type of actions you start taking, you will start manifesting things that you desire, almost without fail.

I am a strong believer that when you start changing things in one area of your life, other areas of your life automatically experience a shift due to the momentum you have created within yourself.

This brings me to a few words of caution: if you currently have toxic people around you, by the end of this book, you will be guaranteed to spend less and less time with them. You might even lose them as friends forever. However, as your mindset changes, you will also attract people that align with your vision. This is completely natural.

It sounds so simple. Why don't more people talk about it?

This is because Personal Development is simple, but it is not easy. As I mentioned earlier, most people are happy with the way things are.

Putting in hours of studying, listening to audio tapes, and reading books that do not involve fast-paced plots are taxing to them. Unless you have a burning desire to take control of your life, this stuff will not mean much to you.

You will also soon start to realize that because of the resistance created in social circles from talking about Personal Development, even people who are dedicated to developing themselves do not like to talk about it.

It is safe to say that, for most people, PD is not the best topic to discuss over a few drinks.

In my opinion, it is ok to talk about PD when you are with company. However, if most of your social circle is resistant to talking about it, it is better to keep it to yourself and find another circle that appreciates such topics.

Quiz 1.

1. What is Personal Development?

   A. A chapter from the Bible
   B. New Age philosophy
   C. Anything that helps you enhance your life
   D. An employee growth initiative

2. Personal Development will...

   A. bring me instant satisfaction
   B. help me win the lottery
   C. equip me to deal with life in a productive manner
   D. stop problems from ever occurring

3. Becoming a better version of yourself...

   A. is not important
   B. is a conscious choice and a lifelong process
   C. frankly, sounds boring. Where is my bag of Cheetos?
   D. is impossible because of circumstances acting against you

4. The following is an example of PD:

   A. Learning to change oil in your car watching YouTube videos
   B. Following a weight lifting program to gain muscle mass
   C. Working on your resume
   D. Staying away from negative people
   E. All of the above

SECTION II

In this section, we will be exploring thinking patterns that keep us from experiencing the world and reaching our goals in a positive, joyous way.

Limiting Beliefs

These are deep-rooted beliefs that force us to live a life that lacks fulfillment. Decisions made under the influence of these beliefs do not allow individuals to become the best version of themselves.

Since our early childhood, we receive many negative messages that we internalize as adults. These messages when coped with badly, result in self-sabotage during adulthood.

Sometimes blatantly harmful e.g. constantly getting in trouble with the law because you internalized the message you heard growing up, "You will never amount to anything." Other times subtle but destructive nonetheless e.g., never taking the SATs because of the belief "No one in my family made it past high school. I surely won't go to college." Limiting beliefs are at the core of criminality and despair.

Limiting beliefs come in all shapes and sizes, some are as destructive as the thoughts in the examples, others are waiting for the right time to become equally as bad. In either case, the results generally ensure that one does not live up to their full potential.

As children, we have grand visions for the future. Limiting beliefs is what guarantees that the same dream and visions for us as adults are nothing but infantile megalomania.

This is because as we age, we start relying too much on our ego. As a result, we worry about looking good in other people's eyes, and we fear falling off our perceived social status. We try to fit in, to conform to mainstream culture. We try to supplicate to the norms of society, and we forget that we once had a dream for ourselves.

We disassociate ourselves from that dream because we fear being labeled a 'pariah', chasing after it. So, we reject the possibility of greatness, fearing the potential of isolation.

We see examples of people that are larger than life on a daily basis, people such as Oprah Winfrey, Bill Gates, Dalai Lama, Nelson Mandela, Warren Buffet, Steve Jobs. However, no sooner are we done reading about or watching a documentary on them, we convince ourselves that such feats are impossible for us.

We pedestalize greatness and look in awe at the contributions made to the world by others, silently dismissing the possibility of us adding massive value to others and being recognized for it.

We blame this on a cornucopia of external reasons. Rarely does the list of alibis contain the real reason, our own limiting beliefs.

Limiting beliefs are also statements that we tell ourselves that convince us that there are disaster and peril on the other side of risk.

Limiting beliefs are the reason we will never be able to give freely to the world the gift that we are meant to give.

Example:

Sarah, a painter by choice is extremely passionate about painting, but watches opportunities pass her by, because she does not think her art is good enough for a large show.

She is resentful of those who get their paintings displayed at galas in front of a large and diverse audience.

In actuality, it takes a lot of effort even for great artists to be showcased at high profile fundraisers. Sarah, owing to her perfectionistic attitude, always feared rejection and is never persistent in her actions to be showcased at such events.

Her limiting belief of "My painting is not good enough for galas" holds her back from the effort required to be showcased at prominent venues.

Exercise:

Identify at least 3 limiting beliefs in your life that may be holding you back and make a note of them in your journal.

If you do not have at least one limiting belief, please consider asking for a refund, as this book may not be for you (or just dig a little deeper maybe)!

Paucity Thinking/ Scarcity Mindset

This is a belief that the universe has limited resources, hence you will never have enough of what you want out of life. Scarcity Mindset is the most prominent form of Limiting beliefs. It is so prominent that it deserves its own section.

A good example of this mindset is, "I will never have enough doing what I love to do because it is not possible to do what I do and make a living."

Our mind hides Paucity Thinking very well, even from ourselves. I am sure we all know at least one person that "borrows" a pen from work and never returns it. It is not the mere act of stealing here that I am pointing to, *but the deep-rooted belief that encourages such an action.*

By habitually "borrowing" the pen, never to return it, one is sending signals to the universe as well as to their subconscious mind that they never have enough money to spare for a pen.

This type of thought is dangerous as it trains the subconscious mind to think small.

The borrower of the pen almost always knows that the pen will never be returned, but feels compelled to bring it home. This is because the borrower of the pen has internalized this negative belief.

Another good example is during salary negotiations. It never fails to amaze me how many people low ball themselves during salary negotiations, just because they believe what they want is a ridiculous amount.

Moreover, they feel that they will automatically lose the opportunity just by asking for what they think they deserve, even though what they may have in mind is the industry standard. No consideration is paid to the fact that if an employer has no room for negotiations in salary, the work experience is probably going to equally inflexible.

Maybe if they asked for what they think they deserved with an open mind, instead of lowballing themselves, there would be no need to "borrow" the pen!

Exercise:

Do you or anyone you know constantly lowballs themselves during salary negotiations?

Do you suspect that Scarcity Mindset is behind it?

Make this an entry in your journal.

Illusion of Action

Working hard at everything except what will ensure your lasting success is the Illusion of Action.

Allow me to explain. We all know someone who is constantly busy, complains that he or she is tired from work, comes home and crashes on the couch in front of the TV. Or someone who is always frantically running around like a chicken with its head cut off, waiting for things to get better.

These are also the people that never cease to tell others how much their job sucks, but they do absolutely nothing to improve their situations.

The Illusion of Action holds a tremendous amount of people hostage because they are almost always busy, yet they have nothing to show for the time spent.

The Illusion of action also shows up in people's dating lives. It can be seen where one of the parties is constantly sending walls of text to the disinterested party, hoping to strike a conversation.

That is action, no doubt, but it's just not helping their cause!

Inaction/Negative Action

Inaction is the complete lack of action towards developing yourself and Negative Action is an action that takes place to ensure that the future is decidedly worse than the present condition.

An example of a Negative Action is the people that constantly binge on Netflix and update their status on social media to brag about it, completely oblivious to what they owe themselves and to the world.

Engaging in mindless consumption of media, although it looks and sounds benign on the outside, is a sure way to take away from the valuable and finite pool of time that we have on this planet.

Inaction and negative action generally go hand in hand. Getting hammered every Saturday and spending all Sunday nursing a headache is a perfect example of this.

Choosing company that enables your own addictive behaviors is another good example of negative action.

While we are talking about Negative action/Inaction and the Illusion of action, I must mention that it is almost impossible for us to achieve goals when our actions are not aligned with them.

Engaging in mindless habits, such as the one I mentioned earlier, not only wastes valuable time, it also takes our mind off our goals.

There is a chapter on Purpose and Goals in the next section, cross reference it later for more.

Exercise:

What kind of illusion of actions/inaction or Negative Action can you identify in yourself?

Can you tell if a Limiting Belief is the root of this? Make a note of this answer; you will be using it later.

Quiz 2

1. The following is an example of a Limiting Belief:

    A. "I am not good enough for that position."
    B. "Whatever, why bother eating healthy? The weight will come right back anyway."
    C. "Circumstances have never favored me. Why would they this time?"
    D. All of the above

2. Scarcity Mindset is...

    A. A recommended plan to deal with lack of finances
    B. A great mindset, especially if you are rich
    C. A sure way to limit yourself by eliminating measured risk from your life.

3. The illusion of Action is...

    A. A brilliant way to avoid doing work, undetected
    B. doing too much, but never anything worthwhile
    C. the idea behind, specific, Massive Action.

4. The following is an example of Negative Action:

    A. going wine tasting South of France.
    B. getting drunk every Friday night and nursing the hangover until late Saturday.
    C. occasionally watching a movie at the cinemas.

5. The following is not an example of Scarcity Mindset:

    A. "I will not gamble more than $50 when I go to Vegas."
    B. "Ambitions are inherently perilous."

C. "I will never spend my money. I'll save for a rainy day"
D. "Charity work is a pathetic way to waste money."

Negative Mindset

This is a mindset that does not allow one to see anything good whatsoever within their lives and outside of it.

The inability to stay in the present moment is largely the reason behind this mindset. Jealousy, unconditional hatred, lack of gratitude and a victim mentality are also at the core of this mindset.

This is by far the most toxic mindsets of all.

It is best to cut all contact with people that display Negative Mindset. Trying to reason with people that have a negative mindset will only work against your sanity.

It is also important to stay away from people that shun your progress, or the positive change in you.

It is to be noted that, Negative Mindset is equally as contagious and as prevalent as the Scarcity Mindset. However, they are more destructive in terms of the effect that they have on us.

Consequently, the first step to positive thinking is to adopt a neutral mindset, if adopting a positive mindset outright is difficult.

Exercise:

Think of a real-life example of a Negative Mindset you have encountered, either in yourself or in the ones closest to you.

How destructive or toxic has it been to you or to others?

I will discuss "going neutral" as a shift away from Negative Mindsets in the next section. Take a few minutes to think of what "going neutral" may mean to you in this context.

Could you think of a scenario that you might benefit from by "going neutral"? Don't bother skipping to the next section, just try and answer with what you have.

Approval Seeking/ People Pleasing

Approval Seekers / People Pleasers derive their sense of self-worth from the people they seek approval from/from people they are trying to please.

Both of these patterns are a form of covert manipulation. People Pleasing as well as Approval Seeking is toxic because the behaviors associated with them are not genuine. Rather, they are an indirect ploy to receive something from the other in exchange.

Approval Seekers, like People Pleasers, derive their sense of self-worth from other people's opinions.

Both mentalities stem from a lack of self-esteem and are particularly perilous for the person that carries the trait. It is to be noted that one can do serious harm to one's self-esteem by depending on another person's approval of themselves.

Completely letting go of Approval Seeking and People Pleasing should be a high priority for individuals that are on the path of Personal Development.

One can never live a happy, joyous, and prosperous life when one is constantly seeking a pat on the back from others.

It is simply impossible for one to people please their way out of life's problems.

While engaging in such behaviors, people either treat you like a doormat or find out that you are inauthentic and avoid you altogether.

These dysfunctions create an increasing chasm of unfulfilled life goals that ultimately lead to immense resentment and distrust of people. A perpetual sense of victimhood soon follows.

Victim Mentality

Victim Mentality is the result of attributing a lack of success to a plethora of external events, but never to one's own tendency of self-sabotage.

A good example of a victim mentality is someone that blames their parents' lack of financial success as a cause of their own poverty filled existence.

This person refuses to look at their own patterns of limiting beliefs that are stopping them from having the type of life they think they deserve.

Victim mentality can often be seen in a person who points out that the people that have made millions from scratch had it way better than they did, totally disregarding any kind of work that goes into making millions.

To further expand on the set of examples, Victim Mentality can also be seen when a guy or a girl constantly complains about having a non-existent dating life to anyone who lends them an ear.

These are the same people that complain about attracting psychos or unfaithful people to them all the time. They fail to realize that no quality person wants to date someone who lacks an overall development of the mind, body, and soul. The principle of "you attract who you are" is completely lost on them.

Finding a scapegoat for all of the life's problems is a common trait among people with Victim Mentality.

Anxiety and Depression

Numerous reasons can be cited as a cause of Anxiety and Depression, but they all boil down to one fact: Anxiety and Depression occur due to a person's inability to stay in the present moment.

Anxiety is the fear of the future. Depression is the inability to isolate the present from the past.

When one suffers from Anxiety and Depression, one loses track of what is in front of them at the present. Because of this, mindful action becomes a mere afterthought.

There was a point in my life when I personally started experiencing crippling anxiety and anxiety-induced panic attacks. I never thought I was going to get over this condition. The mental chatter of negative, anxious thoughts.

This was because I had severe Approval Seeking/People Pleasing tendencies because of which, I allowed my self-worth to hinge on people that couldn't care any less about me.

However, I am grateful that I experienced these panic attacks. It was this experience that compelled me to find a way to get complete control over my life. It is the reason I write this book for everyone: so, they can find a simple way to cope with life's problems.

It is important to note that everyone experiences Anxiety and Depression at some point in their lives. I will tell you that the physical pain of the panic attacks is nothing to reminisce about. However, using the tools that I have laid out in the next section to understand when you are having an anxious thought and to nip it in the bud, is a rewarding experience. Things do get better.

It is possible to overcome Anxiety and Depression without prescription medication. However, in some cases, a carefully doctored dose of Selective Serotonin

Receptor Inhibitors, or SSRIs in addition to medical supervision might be necessary.

After it is all said and done, Anxiety and Depression are at their core a state of mental and physical stagnation. A lack of healthy thought patterns and/or physical activity is both the cause and the effect of these diseases.

The good news is, changing our thought patterns and engaging in physical activity can significantly reduce the effects of these conditions.

Quiz 3

1. Approval Seeking or People Pleasing...

    A. is a sure path to a large social circle that has the same interests as you
    B. is a process successful people have followed for ages
    C. will lower your chances of making a genuine connection with people
    D. is the desired behavior among adults

2. The following is an example of Victim Mentality:

    A. "I will create a life for my children that my parents were unable to provide for me."
    B. "I will never have such a life because I was raised poor."
    C. "No one in my family went to school, but I can certainly change that."
    D. "I will find my purpose."

3. Anxiety and Depression...

    A. stem from the inability to stay in the present moment.
    B. have been eradicated from the United States as of 01/01/2017
    C. is always followed by joy. It's a natural cycle. You cannot always have joy in your life.

INTERMISSION

Congratulations! If you have been reflecting on the topics and engaging in the exercises as laid out in the book so far: You have successfully understood the negative patterns that hold us back from becoming the best version of ourselves.

I also hope that you have been writing in your journal and it has been working well for you.

I want you to pause here for a day or two, and take your time to reflect on what has been said. Re-read a few topics. Your experience will be taken to a whole new level in the next section.

In the section, "What Frees Us," I talk about several methods that one can use for Personal Development. If you are suffering from any of the conditions I mentioned in Section II "Negative patterns that hold us back," don't worry. You will find plenty of tools there to free yourself from what's keeping you hostage.

Once you embark on this journey of shedding the baggage that wears you out, you will discover your authentic self.

You will start noticing the small changes that happen within you before anyone else does. That will be the fuel to your fire. By the time others comment on the changes you have experienced, you would have become a whole new person.

You will have a lighthearted approach to life, yet will be driven to succeed. Your motivation will skyrocket. I hope you carefully work on the next section, taking your time and contemplating what I say.

I will also reiterate that any resistance you come across during any of the topics is OK; find a will to work with it.

Let the fun begin!
Coach KP

SECTION III

If you took a break from the book as recommended, I hope the journal is working wonders for you!

We are on a great run here. After learning about what holds us back, get ready to explore endless opportunities by learning new patterns that help you reach a whole new level of fulfillment.

After this section is completed, you would have a complete understanding of mindsets that are healthy and conducive to growth. You will find techniques to incorporate these concepts into your daily life so that you can deal with stress better and find the motivation to give to the world what you came here to give.

I recommend that you make full use of the Journal that you started. Remember, all emotions need to be processed, and a journal is your best friend if you want to have a healthy relationship with yourself and others.

Healing Your Inner Child

All of us have an inner child within us. Sometimes this inner child is known as your "authentic self" or "true self." The inner child sits still, watching us move through life, without interruption.

However, the inner child is involved in our decision making in a subtle but sure way. To make any lasting progress in Personal Development, healing the inner child is *a necessity.*

Our early experiences--between the time of our birth to puberty— shape our inner child. Due to adverse experiences, sometimes our inner child becomes neglected or wrongfully treated. The hurt and the neglect that the inner child goes through shows up in the form of Self-Doubt, Self-Hatred, and Self-Denial. To release these patterns of self-sabotage, working on our inner child must be the first step towards becoming the best version of ourselves.

Healing the inner child, however, is not a complex process once we understand that all it wants is to be loved and nurtured.

It is unfortunate that most people go their entire lives without knowing about the inner child. However, you are now in the position to be able to heal yours. I have an exercise at the end of this lecture for you to go through so you can find and heal it.

As you do the exercise that follows and start paying attention to your inner child, you will start to gain the ability to slow your thoughts down during times of stress. I recommend you observe and journal any intense emotions that you experience.

As you engage in this process, you will start to understand what exactly your inner child needs from you to heal. You will also learn more about why you make decisions the way you make them.

I suggest doing the exercise, journaling, and paying attention to your inner child a few times over a period of several days before moving to the next lecture. This is important stuff!

Exercise:

Read from your journal and locate some of the dates and times when you experienced negative emotions.

Do you see a pattern? Can you tell why you experienced them?

Was it your own feelings that were making you go through this experience? Or was it something that someone else said or did?

If you have no journal yet, I recommend you start a journal and come back to this section once you have at least 10 entries in it.

Inner Child Meditation

Write the script down in your own handwriting, preferably in an in your journal where you will be writing scripts. Additionally, you may record it so you can listen to it when you are on the go.

Find a quiet place. Take deep diaphragm breaths (breaths that fill your abdomen, and then are emptied fully) for a minute and read the script (out loud if possible) or listen to the script that you recorded, repeating the words and continuing to take deep breaths. Repeat this at least 20 times twice a day for a month, all the while contemplating that you are having a conversation with your inner child. Write down the emotions that you experience right before and right after the meditation. This is important.

Observe any resistance that comes up as you practice the script. If you are absolutely unable to repeat it word for word for whatever reason, feel free to modify it. However, you must come back to the script at some point to completely heal your inner child.

Script:

"Dear Inner Me, I send love and gratitude to you. You are loving, lovable and loved. The hurt that you have experienced is understood and acknowledged. The love I send you is healing the wounds and a new sense of joy and gratitude is replacing the hurt you have felt in the past. You are now protected and safe in this space. All is whole and complete."

Once you complete 30 days of this meditation, you can come back to this script. Add to it or modify it and continue this meditation as it suits you.

Loving Yourself and Receiving Love

From an early age, we are taught to love our neighbors and be nice to our guests, to give unconditional love to our significant others and to our children. However, we rarely learn that we first need to love ourselves unconditionally to be able to fully love anyone else.

Lack of self-love pushes us to seek love from external sources, often by engaging in approval seeking and people pleasing behaviors. By doing so, we are not only denying ourselves unconditional love but also are projecting to the world that we are unworthy of it. This is a terrible place to be in.

A deep-rooted problem such as this one can only be resolved by practicing Self-Love. As we practice Self-Love, we start expanding our ability to feel love. We begin to accept kindness from others, without compulsively doing anything for them in return.

Notice that I said Self-Love is a practice. Like any other concept in Personal Development, making something second nature takes time and effort.

Also, note that Self-Love does not mean narcissism. By practicing self-love, one becomes more compassionate towards others, and not the other way around. Acts of self-aggrandization are not acts of Self-Love; neither is constantly talking about yourself and your accomplishments.

Self-Love is a practice where you nurture your mind, body, and soul.

Self-Love is the habit of owning mistakes you have made without beating yourself up for them.

Self-Love is standing up for yourself.

Self-Love is understanding that an area of your life that needs work does not define you.

Self-Love is the knowledge that the results of past failures do not define you.

Self-Love is believing in yourself when nobody else believes in you.

Self-Love is being OK making a choice and sticking to it.

Self-Love is taking action in presence of doubt.

Self-Love is not profusely apologizing to everyone for making a mistake in your life.

Self-Love is learning from your mistakes, but not dwelling on them.

Once you love yourself unconditionally, you will begin to receive unconditional love. Only at that point will loving others unconditionally be possible.

Exercise:

Look at yourself in a mirror. Observe your face. Look in the eyes of your own image and say, "I love you". Take some time to observe yourself. Watch the emotions that stir up. Note them down.

Practice this routine daily, until you are filled with positive emotions. If the resistance here is very high, try looking at the bottom of your reflection and move up as you start to feel more comfortable.

This mirror work is known to bring out intense emotions in the first attempt. Stick with it. There will come a time when you will be completely OK with this practice.

Releasing SDHD

SDHD: Self Doubt, Self-Hatred, Self-Denial.

SDHD is the result of chronic malignant mental conditioning. The doubt, hatred, and denial of the Self go hand in hand. These conditions stem from a general belief of, "I am not good enough".

Self-Doubt is the act of constantly doubting yourself. When suffering from Self-Doubt, it is hard to take a definite action. Even when one does manage to take action, one is unable to fully experience the process due to a prevailing sense of anxiety of having made the wrong decision.

Internalizing messages such as a variation of "You cannot do anything right," over a course of time lead to Self-Doubt.

Spending time with people that are not appreciative of your goals, dreams, and desires is the number one reason for Self-Doubt for most people. Equally high on the list are toxic parenting and schooling.

Self-Hatred is a complete dislike of the self. It stems from comparing ourselves to others, or to an ideal self, and not finding our lives up to the perceived standards of perfection. Self-hatred leads to addictive behavior, as one starts to find solace in seeing themselves through a lens of fantasy.

Self-Denial is a chronic state of cognitive dissonance; where the outward projection of one's self is not in accord with the inward authentic self. This is when one intensely tries to fit into what he or she thinks is "normal," hence restricting one's authentic self from radiating onto the world.

Self-Denial causes severe conflict by pitting who you are against the person you want others to perceive you as. Because of this, people go through a destructive mental tug of war, that holds them from bringing their purpose(s) of life to fruition.

SDHD collectively destroys confidence and robs us from the joys of life.

To release SDHD, we must come to terms with the fact that we are unique beings, and all of us have our own sets of strengths and weaknesses. This is a simple concept, yet is not an easy one to fully comprehend, especially when suffering from SDHD.

If you suffer from SDHD, give yourself permission to not succeed overnight, and focus on the rest of this section. If you don't, it is still a worthy read.

Trying to fit in is a perilous way to live life. Life is a joyous experience only when we belong to ourselves.

Steps to Release SDHD

When we find ourselves bogged down by Self-Doubt, we need to understand and acknowledge what is exactly happening to us. The decisions that we must make, should be made while acknowledging the presence of the doubt.

We must allow that the decision we are making, in light of the facts present in front of us, can be wrong, yet still, proceed with the decision. *This is the key to release self-doubt.*

When we release the need to be right all the time, Self-Doubt vanishes. There is no one in this world that has not made mistakes. Not making a decision owing to Self-Doubt is also a decision, albeit a worse one.

There is no correct formula for winning all the time. *We must internalize that making mistakes is a part of life and that the* decisions that we make, do not define us.

Comparing our weakest moments and vulnerabilities with what others portray on the outside is what leads us to Self-Hatred. By the virtue of living with ourselves 24/7, we know ourselves more than anyone else on the planet ever can. When we compare ourselves to others, most of the time, we are comparing our weaknesses to their strengths. By doing this, we are setting ourselves up for failure.

There is no way for us to know what the vulnerabilities and weaknesses of other people are, in a way that we know our own. People do not put weaknesses on display; what is often on display is a well-curated portrait. This is a fact of life.

Comparison of this sort is pointless and toxic. If Self-Hatred is stopping our success, we need to uproot that mindset and cultivate Self-Compassion. *Practicing Self-Compassion, and ceasing to compare ourselves to others, is the only way to recover from Self-Hatred.*

Self-Denial stems from not allowing our authentic self to reflect on the outside. The cause is rooted in the belief that, "If we allow them to see who I am on the inside, they will never love me".

One comes off as fake and inauthentic while one operates in the mode of self-denial. Even if we somehow mask our authentic self extremely well, our dreams, goals, values will always be shadowed by what others find more desirable. In the long run, one can only hide their true self from themselves and the world for so long.

To wipe out Self-Denial from our life, we must cultivate a mindset of belonging to ourselves, rather than fitting in with a group.

When we live an authentic life, people that value you as a person will flock to you. People that do not, and are in your life just because they see you as a different person than you really are, will leave. Good riddance!

The Purpose of Life and Goal-setting

All of us bring unique gifts to the world. To prosper and live a truly fulfilled life, we must first find what this gift is and then find a way to deliver this gift to the world, this is the Purpose of Life.

In order to fulfill our purpose, we must become fruitful. Becoming fruitful means producing more than you need for yourself. In other words, your purpose should be larger than just you.

Discovering the true purpose (or, potentially, purposes) of life takes some work. Sometimes, we go all over looking for the purpose of our lives, only to find out that it was right under our noses the entire time.

Other times, we must literally travel the world and climb mountains to discover it. When we find that which gives us unconditional joy and fulfillment, we have discovered our purpose.

Most of the time, the purpose of our life is already known to us. It is what we have always been good at, since our childhood. It is what we could spend hours doing, without the expectation of riches or recognition. It is something we love to do so much that everything else is secondary to it.

Money, Fame, and Recognition are the byproducts of perfecting your craft. That larger than yourself aspect of a purpose will by definition ensure that you receive your fair share of accolades. The trick is to not get too hung up on the results and continue working towards that purpose. Once the cup is full, the water will overflow and drench what surrounds the cup, this is inevitable.

For me, what brings me true joy is teaching others what I have learned through experience, sharing my stories and adventures, and listening to the trials and tribulations of others. I can do this without the expectations of gains. This is the purpose of my life.

I also believe that if I am able to help enough people become a better version of themselves, then enough people will help me become the better version of myself. It is classic Law of Attraction at play.

We all have purposes that vary in nature. We must not start comparing purposes, for no purpose is small or big, right or wrong. Once a purpose in life is discovered, we need to work to ensure that we don't lose track of it.

Purpose of Life vs Goals

I often get asked if our goals are our purpose of life. I believe that goals are different from the purpose of life, for goals can be set for various reasons that may or may not be in alignment with our purpose.

However, if our goals closely align with the purpose of our lives, reaching those goals help us excel at our purpose. Everything becomes synchronous at that point.

Often, goals are set for the sole purpose of enjoying the results. However, goal setting should be a mindful task, and must not be in direct conflict with our inner self or the purpose of our life.

Life has various facets. Goal setting and working in alignment with the purpose of our life makes these facets more harmonious. Creating a life around our purpose is the best gift we can give to ourselves.

On occasion, the purpose of our life can change, depending on what period of our lives we are in. If we suddenly find ourselves staring at a new purpose in life, we must pay close attention to the motive for the switch.

Jumping from one purpose to the other at whim, or because the first purpose was boring or difficult, only means that the true purpose of life may not yet have been discovered.

Purpose Finding and
Goal Setting Exercises:

Do you know your purpose of life? What is it?

Why do you think this is your purpose?

Could there be other purposes that might replace this purpose for you?

If you have not yet found a purpose in life, then how do you intend to find it?

What is it that you truly enjoy, without expectation of tangible or intangible benefits? Could this be your purpose? If not, why?

Write down two goals that you have for the next six months. If you do not have any, don't panic. Start thinking about what you can accomplish in the next six months to a year that will bring you joy. Write it down.

If you do not have goals, then ask yourself why that is. Is it because you are waiting for something to happen for you to set goals?

If you have goals, are they in alignment with your purpose?
Remember, it is not mandatory for each goal to align with the purpose of your life. In what ways can you modify your goal to better align with your purpose?

Write all of the answers down and review them in 3 weeks, 6 weeks, 3 months and 6 months' time. Note the progress you have made at each review.

Gratitude & Forgiveness Practice

In your journey to becoming the best version of yourself, you will find that there are many people that have helped you in one way or the other. You will also recall that there are plenty of characters that have hindered your growth and hurt you. You will need to find a way to practice being grateful to people that you owe gratitude towards and forgive the ones that have done you wrong.

Gratitude practice allows us to take the time to thank the people that have had a positive impact on our lives. For various reasons, we are not always able to fully thank people that have helped us. Gratitude practice ensures that your gratitude is sent to them--directly or indirectly—via the universe. Physical presence is not a necessity to express gratitude and forgiveness.

We also spend time thinking negative thoughts about people that have hurt us. In return, we lose our ability to move forward with our lives. Forgiveness is the only way to let go of anger and resentment, making space for peace and prosperity in life.

Forgetting the wrongs that were done to us is not a necessary part of forgiveness practice. Forgiveness is essential for us to break free from the shackles of resentment. Any resentment towards others is a barrier to personal growth and success. It is the equivalent of drinking poison and hoping the other person dies. Forgiveness is the antidote to resentment.

Gratitude Meditation

Use the following script as a meditation to express gratitude and let go of resentment. As usual, handwrite this script or record it in your own voice to listen to it.

This script should be used after the inner child meditation, or any time positive or, especially, negative emotions arise about a certain person.

Script

"I am grateful for having ___, ___, _____ in my life. I love spending time with them and I wish them all the best in their journey. I thank my higher power for the opportunity that I have been given to learn and grow as a person due to my interaction with them. I bring in love to myself and send love to _____, _____, ___ ."

As you mature with the script, feel free to add to it or modify it to your liking. You will find that as you mature, you may even be able to send gratitude to people that hurt you, for they are the ones that pushed you to grow!

Forgiveness Meditation

Instructions for Gratitude Practice applies.

Script

"_____,_____,_____. I forgive you for the wrongs you have done to me. I hope you find the courage to forgive yourself as well. The hurt that you put me through has healed and I see a wonderful future ahead of me. All is well in my world."

At first, you might meet resistance in forgiving those that have not been kind to you in the past. Just remember that to develop as a person, it is important to start doing things differently.

Mindfulness Practice

Most of the people that struggle with life, struggle from their inability to stay in the present moment. A wandering mind is often involved in lamenting about the past or worrying about the future.

Mindfulness which is at the core of Buddhism is a cure to such worries. For this reason, in the West, it is synonymous to the ability to "stay in the present moment".

Anxiety, Depression and many other negative mindsets emerge from a lack of mindfulness. The natural state of mind, where it is the most productive, is when it is present in the current slice of time, without the fear of the future or contemplation of the past.

You may know, especially if you have been writing in the journal for a while now, that the action of writing your feelings down brings you immense relief. One of the reasons behind this is that creating scripts on paper with a pen, and watching the ink make an impression on paper, allows us to take our mind off the past and the future and makes us concentrate on the task at hand.

Meditation and consciously feeling your feelings are both mindfulness practices. Listening to other people talk, really paying attention to what is being said, is also a form of mindfulness. Mindfulness also means engaging in our day to day activities with presence and conviction.

We live in a world that overstimulates our senses every step of the way. We gather information from a myriad of sources that may not necessarily be beneficial to our growth. The natural tendency after receiving information is to try to process it. Such activities hinder mindfulness, just as excessive multitasking takes away from our experience to truly feel an experience as it unfolds.

Due to the presence of numerous electronic distractions, practicing Mindfulness to learn being mindful in our day to day life has never been as necessary as today.

I have found a simple but powerful mindfulness practice that I have listed under below. Personally, when I feel anxiety in my body, I use a variation of this strategy to come back to the present moment. This mindfulness meditation practice is sure to help you.

Exercise:

Find a textured object that you can fit between your thumb and the index finger; it could be a raisin, a coin, or a pebble. I will use a coin as an example for the exercise.

Find a quiet place where you can relax without disturbances.

Observe the head side of the coin while breathing deeply. Really pay attention to every specific detail on the face of the coin, the head, the textures of the hair, the nose, the engravings etc.

Do this for ten full breaths, then flip the coin and observe the symbols and the writings on the tail side. Feel free to name each of the symbols and read any words to yourself during this observation.

Feel the weight of the coin between your fingertips. The texture on the side of the coin. The color and any scuffs or age marks on it.

In your journal, write down how you felt about the experience. As you mature in this practice, you will find ways to perform this meditation even with no coin or a prop but the texture of your fingers alone.

Feel free to add to or modify this exercise once you are comfortable with it.

Keeping a Journal/Writing

No matter how trivial an emotion is, it needs to be fully experienced, or else the emotion stays locked inside the body, causing us stress and physical ailments.

To experience and process our emotions safely, we need a safe outlet. Having a close friend or family members to talk to certainly helps. However, I find it inconvenient and cumbersome to recruit a friend for every little thing I like to discuss. I also find it unfair to make anyone listen to negative emotions every time we experience them.

Journaling has the advantage of being inexpensive, and almost always available, it is as discreet as you want it to be, and can provide you company at any hour of the day. It's a win-win situation. Many people that pay exorbitant fees to get counseling could easily shave half of the face-time with their counselors just by using a journal.

Writing things down is also important for tracking your progress. It is a wonderful feeling to see what your feelings were at this exact time in the past week, month or year, and how much progress has been made since. It is also very satisfying to see how your problems have evolved-- along with your abilities to cope with them.

For these reasons, journaling is a very important tool that we need to immediately start leveraging. I personally do not believe that the structure of how a journal is written is as important as the content of the journal itself.

If you find yourself without your Journal, scribbling things on a piece of paper and transferring them to the Journal as soon as you can, works just as well.

However, I strongly recommend new users to use a pocket Journal and to always keep it handy.

Other outlets could be writing poems or articles, or else letters to your future or past self, to people you have a relationship with, letters asking for forgiveness, letters of forgiveness, etc. It is not necessary to mail these pieces of writings.

I know from personal as well as professional contacts with clients that writing things down in your own handwriting trumps the use of digital devices by far. The chances of distractions are minimal and seeing your own handwriting at work makes for a much-enhanced experience.

I recommend you maintain a physical Journal and refrain from using digital devices.

Three Breaths of Consciousness

This exercise is meant to be a quick nudge to bring your wandering mind back to the present moment. However, it is not designed to replace your mindfulness/meditation practice.

Beginners that do not practice mindfulness or other traditional meditation on a regular basis can use this practice to build a meditation foundation. This works wonders for people who have resistance towards meditation by letting them see the benefits of extending three breaths to a regular, extended meditation practice.

Exercise:

When you are out and about, dealing with the regular stresses of life, such as in a meeting with a client, or driving, you may find that locating a quiet space or writing in your Journal is not possible. Use the following simple and short process to bring your mind to the present.

Take a deep breath paying extra attention to your nostrils as you inhale, following the breath down the throat and through the esophagus. Feel the lungs filling with air. Once the lung is completely full, hold the breath for a second, all the while noticing the inflation in the lungs. Exhale slowly, following the train of air from the lungs, to the windpipe, to the head, and out of the nostrils. Repeat this three times.

If you are experiencing immense stress or anxiety at the moment, you may need to repeat this process a few times before you can entirely come to the present moment.

For beginners, this is a great way to get into meditation. This is also one of those rare things in Personal Development that will give you instant results. Use it to your benefit!

Cultivating an Abundance Mentality

Scarcity Mindset or Paucity Thinking is driven by the principle that we cannot have anything good in our lives because the amount of good out there is finite. Scarcity Mindset effectively stops us from putting effort into anything worthwhile.

Abundance Mentality is an antidote to such a belief system. The principle of Abundance Mentality is that the universe has plenty of resources for us all. With the right mindset and specific actions, we can achieve what we were meant to achieve and give to the world what we came here to give.

Abundance Mentality is also very important in the process of letting go. Without Abundance Mentality, we tend to hold on to people, positions, and events from the past for a very long time, harboring resentment and guilt from various episodes. Abundance Mentality frees us from these toxic bonds and allows us to give a 100% towards our goals and purpose.

Once you understand and feel that there is plenty for everyone, the need to cling to unhealthy items from the past vanishes.

To achieve success, a certain level of measured risk taking is required. Taking risks under the influence of scarcity is an impossible task to accomplish. However, cultivating an abundance mentality makes it easier to take measured risks, regardless of your present situation.

Even if we don't see results after acting, the lessons learned from our actions are valuable in our lives. Abundance mentality and action teaches us an important lesson that failing to achieve success in one shot is not failure; it is a part of life.

Abundance Mentality enables us to see the positive side of things and focus on ways to achieve, rather than compulsively finding faults and never attempting to reach our goals. It is essential to understand that it is what we focus that will grow.

One thing to note is that Abundance Mentality is not a license for reckless behavior. We need to ensure that our actions are deliberate and consistent with our goals and purpose. Caution must be exercised in order to stay away from Negative Action or the Illusions of Action.

Owning Our Experiences

"I am a sole creator of my experience." Please write this down in your journal. Every time you feel like pointing a finger at someone for the setbacks you face, remember it.

With an exception of our childhood, we are at least partially responsible for the things that happen to us throughout the rest of our life. There is no exception to this rule.

Yes, some of what we experience is entirely undesirable, and there are times when things happen to us against our will. This, we must acknowledge, along with the fact that life is not fair.

However, even in a situation where we seemingly lack total control of the events around us, we must own our reaction to them. This comes with an understanding that *we can control our reactions to external events*.

We may find that it is easy to own our experience when positive and rewarding things happen to us. However, when undesirable things happen, it is easier to resort to finger pointing and playing the victim.

A true test of character occurs when things go against our will. Owning our experience during such times means understanding the part we played in the situation. It is not an easy thing to do, however, it is an important part of never allowing the undesirable experience to happen again.

Inability to own your experience results in pity begging, and perpetual self-victimization. This may even work out for us in the short term in the form of attention from others. But the fact is that the addictive nature of the attention one gets from pity begging and self-victimization opens one up to experience further hurt & victimization.

Owning our experience is the only way to bring progress in life and to break away from the addictive, self-sabotaging nature of self-victimization.

Exercise:

Think of an example of a time where you owned a negative experience that you had and decided to never have it again.

Can you think of someone who perpetually victimizes themselves for attention? Do you see this trend on social media?

Imagine this experience: You are halfway through a big project and your laptop is stolen, and all your data was on the laptop. How do you own your experience in this case?

How do you think you should react when you see others not owning their experiences? (Hint: You can only control your own reactions)

Harnessing the Power of Positive Thinking and Affirmations

One of the major tenets of personal development is that *We are what we attract*. Negative Mindset, as described in an earlier section, is a sure way to receive negative results. If we are constantly in a negative frame of mind with regards to ourselves and of others, it is a foregone conclusion that our life is not headed in a positive direction.

We get conditioned by stimulus outside of ourselves from an early age to see and respond to the negative. A 5-minute stroll through the news channels should confirm this. Positive Thinking is something we must cultivate to undo the footprint of such Negative stimuli and to counter our innate negativity bias.

How to Cultivate Positive Thinking

Engaging in Positive Thinking consciously, early on, could make for a difficult process. Feelings of "overdoing it" or "being phony" are often reported by people who first begin this process. The further away from a Positive Mindset you are when starting out, the more your resistance will be towards "Positive Thinking".

Unconditional Self Love and Acceptance and Release of SDHD is pivotal in making Positive Thinking a part of your life. These processes should at least be practiced in parallel.

Having said that, personal experience tells me that this is not a particularly tricky process to manage: All three of these mindsets go hand in hand.

To start out, along with your journal, you will have to pay attention to what comes out of your mouth and the thoughts that generate in your mind.

Exercise:

When you find yourself saying something negative, it is imperative that you **STOP and change the topic.** There is nothing more to it. You do not need to beat yourself up when this happens, but you do need to find a way to stop. Stopping makes you think twice about going negative again. It also allows you to do less damage to your progress by stopping right where you are before the floodgates of negativity open.

It is a good thing from a social standpoint as well.

When you find yourself thinking negative thoughts or having negative emotions, you need to FEEL them. **Do not try to stop** these thoughts. Do not beat yourself for thinking negatively, just stay with the negative emotions and allow them to pass you by.Understand that your thoughts are not who you are. This is actually a great time to pull out your Journal and start writing. Write down exactly what you are feeling at the time. After you have felt your feelings, if you still find yourself being negative, practice the "Three Breaths of Consciousness" exercise from this book.

Going Neutral

Sometimes, it seems impossible to let go of a negative thought. In this case, it is important that you Go Neutral.

For example, if you feel extremely negative about finding the love of your life, instead of saying to yourself, "I will never find anyone, ever. Why try?" try saying, "I believe that it is possible to find someone I can share my life with" until you are ready to say, "I am positive that I will find someone." Going Neutral is leaps and bounds better than staying negative. If you practice this thought process, soon you will surprise yourself by thinking positive at times when you would generally be thinking negative.

All you need to do is Practice, Journal, and Practice some more. Repeat!

Positive Affirmations for Success and Health

Positive Affirmations are best done in the present tense. All the emotions related to already having acquired the object of desire (peace, wealth, health etc.) must be felt during this practice. Feeling the emotions as if they were already true is an inseparable part of using positive affirmations.

You must believe that you have acquired a certain object or achieved a certain goal *before* they get manifested in reality. Just like an architect who designs a building in its entirety on a computer, using design software, you must imagine that you are in possession of what exactly what you want out of life. Having such a visual is necessary for everyone to attain the object of your desire in real life.

Exercise:

Find a quiet place.

Write this script down and/or record it in your own voice and play it back as you repeat the words.

"I love myself. I am loving, lovable and loved. I attract success and prosperity. All of my goals are easy for me to achieve. I am a unique and gifted person. My family and friends love and appreciate my contributions. I love and appreciate my family and friends. I have a wonderful life."

You can add as many of these lines as you would like, for example, if you want affirmations for good health you may add a line such as, "I have a perfect body that enables me to live the type of life I want to experience." As long as the affirmations are positive and in the present tense.

Plow through any resistance that arises during this exercise. The time that you spend repeating affirmations is no time to ask yourself if any of this is true. I strongly believe that negative emotions must be felt, but during the time of affirmation practice, one must try to focus solely on the positive.

If you find yourself really negative during the session, write what you felt in your Journal. Compare that entry to your notes about subsequent affirmation sessions. It will get better.

You will memorize parts or all of this script after repeating the exercises a few times. At that point, you can start the affirmations off with your eyes closed.

I get told sometimes that Positive Thinking is nothing but "feel good nonsense". I think that criticism says volumes about Positive Thinking, I would rather engage in "feel good nonsense" than in nonsense that is counterproductive and makes me feel bad at the same time.

I cannot tell you enough about the importance of Positive Thinking in order to grow as a person. Life becomes grim and joyless without positive thoughts.

Yes, understanding of the negative things in life is important, in order to avoid them. However, authentic joy and lasting success can only be achieved by focusing all your strength on what you want rather than what you do not want. This is an important point. Make note of it.

Setting Emotionally Compelling Goals

We all know at least one person that manages to forget their New Year's resolutions by the 15th of January. We also know people that set goals and quit way before ever attempting to follow through. I have been guilty of such fumbles myself in the past.

This is because we know "What" we want out of those goals, but we do not know "Why" we want them. During goal setting, having an emotionally compelling "Why" is pivotal to a guaranteed "What".

Unless the "Why" is emotionally compelling to us, the "What" will not be of much use to us in our journey.

The stronger the "Why" the more powerful the effort to achieve the "What". Generally, the "What" is easy to find, but the "Why" takes some deep diving.

Some "Whys" can be

"For my family…"
"To prove to myself …"
"To help…"
"For posterity…"
"To cure…"
"To impart knowledge….."

Exercise:

What were some of the emotionally compelling reasons for you to read this book?

Do you have any short or long-term goals? Are there strong "Whys" behind them?

How about your purpose in life? Is there an emotionally compelling reason behind it?

Specific, Massive Action

I know, Specific, Massive Action sounds like a lot of work. So, what really does it mean to take Massive Action?

Massive Action is a deliberate, measured move towards a purpose in life. Massive Action involves reaching specific, emotionally compelling goals that are in line with your purpose.

While committing to a Massive Action plan, the "What," the "When" and the "Why" must be clearly defined. This constitutes a specific, Massive Action plan.

In my personal life, having and committing to Massive Action has helped me more than anything else in achieving my goals.

To give you the logic behind Specific, Massive Actions, here is an example: Think of an idea that gives you goosebumps, that you think will add value to yourself or others, and that you really want to accomplish.

In the world of Massive Action, instead of bouncing this idea around with your friends, or talking to family or your significant other, you would write down the "What, When and the Why" first, and then immediately start working towards your goals. What you are aiming for here, at the minimum, is a prototype or a first draft of what you want to accomplish, before you start to showcase your ideas.

Writing the What, the When and the Why of the Massive Action plan is extremely important because it helps the plan to be specific. Specifying exactly what is desired makes taking action and manifesting the vision that much easier.

Imagine the statement, "I want to earn millions making wheelchairs" vs. "I will earn 10 million dollars by the end of March 2019 by establishing an organization that is dedicated to making 3D printed wheelchairs accessible to the public. I will change the lives of people with disabilities." The difference should speak for itself.

Where Massive Action really helps is to not squander away great ideas by talking about them so much that your enthusiasm deflates. It helps you understand your limitations and challenges you to find creative ways to overcome them.

The momentum you gather with Specific, Massive Action will inspire you further to see the product or the idea that you have in mind come to fruition.

Something to note here is that Massive Action is more than just the initial push for a project, It encompasses the entire timeline of a goal and enhances productivity until a tangible outcome is achieved.

Exercise:

What are some of the areas of your life that could benefit from taking Specific, Massive Action? What are the 3 W's for those ideas? What is the emotionally compelling reason behind them?

Create a Massive Action plan for a goal you want to achieve 6 months from now by defining your 3 W's. Elaborate your plan and write about the emotionally compelling reason (the "Why").

Do you welcome change in life? How does the subject of "Taking Massive Action" make you feel about your goal? What may be holding you back? Can you identify any limiting beliefs? Answer Honestly.

Unleashing the Power of Habit

Today's habits are what makes our future. If you are successful today, I guarantee that you had habits that were conducive to growth in the past. If you are looking for success, then it is imperative that you work towards growth yielding habits.

Positive thinking and any of the mindset improvement techniques that we have discussed in this book so far, are meant to get you to take action. Once you start taking action towards incorporating something in your life, you are engaging in a habit-forming process. It is true that habits take the time to develop. However, it is also true that habits once developed, help us become a better person.

According to the Habit Loop Theory, explained in the book 'The Power of Habit' by Charles Duhigg, Habit is the combination of Cue, Routine, and Reward.

The Cue is what triggers the Routine. It is often compelling, for example, working out right after work, at 5:00 PM. The Routine, the obvious part, is what you wish to change or reinforce: In this case, the workout. The Reward is what provides positive reinforcement for the Routine. In this case, it might be a guilt-free beer, or simply the satisfaction of working out.

Good habits, combined with a correct mindset, make it a breeze to set goals and reach the purpose of your life.

Generally, it takes a person month of daily practice to develop something into a habit. So, the key to turning an action into a habit is practice. Once you understand the components of the Habit Loop, it becomes easier to change it by replacing the routine while keeping the cue and the reward unchanged.

It is important during these formative times to understand that a missed opportunity to carry out the routine does not negate past sequence of progress. It is akin to missing a pill. You take it the next day and try not to miss the next dose. It is also important not to beat yourself up if you should ever fail. If that happens, you must strengthen your resolve and carry on with the routine the next day until a new habit is established.

Forming new habits is the best way to let go of old habits and patterns that no longer serve you.

Stuck doing the same thing that is not yielding you results? Switch the routine, and you won't have to worry about how to quit. It will take practice, and won't necessarily be easy, but it will be doable.

Remember, it's what you pay attention to that grows!

Letting Go!

As human beings that are conditioned to need society to thrive, we often become too attached to processes (e.g. relationships), and substances (e.g. alcohol). We also attach our self-image to some of our attributes (e.g. "I'm a leader"), or external philosophies (e.g. "I'm a hipster").

In the process of getting attached to an object or an idea, we tend to forget our authentic self. The only way to regain the connection to our core is by letting go. We must let go of what does not aid in our growth as a person.

You attract what you are; conversely, you are attracted to what you are. You will have to let go of toxic company once you realize that your personal aspirations are clashing with those around you. You will also realize that letting go of the undesired is the only way to welcome what is desired in your life.

Letting go is not always easy. However, hanging on to the negative is outright toxic. If you hang on to people, places, events, and actions that are not working out for you, you are setting yourself up for further disappointment and failure.

The quickest way to let go of something toxic is to find a healthy replacement.

Letting go is the abundance mindset at its best!

CAUTION:

Unless there is verbal/emotional or physical abuse in a relationship, most problems can be resolved by open communication. Before letting go of important relationships in life, one must exhaust all means of fair communication.

Exercise:

"Letting go" is a concept that can be applied to a wide array of things. The exercise I am going to suggest here is used to let go of past events.

I call this "stadium work."

Find a quiet Place

Imagine an event that you have been having a very hard time letting go of.

For this exercise, I will use an example of a heated argument with a co-worker that is causing you to feel resentment towards him and your job.

Keep taking deep belly breaths throughout this exercise.

Now close your eyes and imagine you are having this argument in the middle of a football field inside a stadium, somewhere close to the center. Notice how it is making you feel. Notice any physical and emotional changes that arise, such as high pulse rate, anxiety, or anger and rate them on a scale of 1 to 10.

From here, Imagine yourself as a bystander watching this from a point on the perimeter of the field. Note your emotions and sensations, as you did earlier.

From here, imagine yourself as a bystander moving further away, this time watching the episode from one of the walls around the field, with the sound of the argument growing weaker. Note your level of mental and physical activity.

From here, imagine yourself watching this argument from a seat in the first row, the visuals and the sound getting ever smaller. Continue to make mental note of those feelings.

Keep moving further up the rows, then to the next level, next, up to the last one. Imagine how the audiovisuals are affecting you less and less as the sound and the visuals become barely visible/audible. In the end, imagine yourself at the last row seats. You cannot hear any of the argument at this point and all you see is a blur. Note your feelings. Have they subsided?

Repeat this exercise as many times as it takes for the strong feelings to turn into something that does not affect you.

This exercise can be modified in order to let go of various things. You may modify it and use it to your liking once you have tried a few different iterations of this exercise. The most important aspect of this practice is that you have to be aware of how your feelings and bodily sensations change as you remove yourself further and further away from the argument.

Your Image

As a part of developing as a person, we need to get into the habit of owning our image by displaying our best self to the world. This includes everything, from the way we dress and the way we shake hands to our posture, the vocabulary that we use, and the knowledge that we carry.

We are all subconsciously judging and being judged by others using these attributes, whether we like it or not. As it is our business to correctly interpret information that we receive from the outside world, It is also our business to regulate what information we project to it.

It is essential to understand that no matter how we choose to look at things, despite our elevated consciousness or our active work towards negating biases, most people still use a mainstream, cultural scale to judge others.

This is not about fitting in, but about marketing yourself. In marketing yourself, you show the aspect that is the most desirable to the demographic that you are aiming to do business with. If milk commercials showed desperate, depressed cows in cages, the milk industry would perish as fast as a gallon of milk left outside the refrigerator!

I am not suggesting that you completely betray yourself. For example, if wearing a suit to a business meeting is totally not your thing, then don't do it. However, what I am pointing out is that your chance of making a deal is much higher if you choose to dress according to standards, or even a notch above them. This is a fact of life.

This brings me to caution the readers against the popular attitude of "keeping it real" and "YOLO." If "keeping it real" and "YOLO" is a part of your persona and you are making a living off of it, more power to you. However, if getting things done, and reaching another level of professional and personal success, is your goal, then "letting it all hang out" might not be the best strategy to get there. Use caution and do not engage in Negative Action.

If you have come this far in the course, I do not believe your goal is to look sloppy, talk with a mouthful of profanity, or engage in meek handshakes. So, take my words for it: The effort you take to make yourself look your best will give you a better chance at succeeding than not.

Always Remember:

Sloppiness is Kryptonite to Personal Development.

SECTION IV

In this section, I recommend some concepts that you can pursue as the next step in your Personal Development Journey.

Nurturing the Mind, Body, and Soul

It is essential while developing yourself to pay attention to the dynamics of the mind, body, and soul.

As you grow and develop as a person, you are bound to hit a plateau. When you feel like something is not working or something could be done better, it is most likely that one of those three areas need work.

There are various ways to work on the mind: reading, learning from others, practicing what is learned, staying away from addictions, etc.

Similarly, there are activities for the body, such as strength training, cardio work, massages, etc. Then there are activities to nurture the soul, such as prayer, meditation, Reiki, energy healing, etc.

One thing to note is that you do not need to be religious to work on your soul. You must cultivate a spirituality that suits you the best. The root of most spirituality, in my opinion, starts with compassion.

Strength Training /Bodybuilding

I decided to make strength training a separate topic because in my teaching experience, as well as in my personal experience, I have yet to find anything that has so many benefits.

Strength training keeps you mindful, helps you visualize growth as a process, encourages you to eat well, teaches you the importance of sticking to a routine to achieve results, improves your posture, and makes your body stronger.

Strength training is great for the release of anxiety and other negative emotions, such as anger and frustration, and does not require a large amount of space. It is not dependent upon the weather, as most strength training can be done in the confines of one room, with very little equipment involved.

I recommend strength training as a tool for runners, hikers, and people that love the outdoors, as well as people that have no experience in working out. When it comes to working your mind body and soul, strength training has it all.

YouTube has some great strength training videos for beginners. Go check them out!

Yoga, Mindfulness, Meditation

Most of the exercises that I have created for this book are mindfulness-based practices. If you have been doing these exercises, you have already started reaping the benefits of staying in the present moment.

For those of you that are interested in the practice of yoga, I suggest that you incorporate self-love affirmations before and after your yoga practice. Yoga is more than just a set of stretching exercises. In the East, the pioneers of yoga always practiced along with lessons in compassion and self-love, and it often went hand-in-hand with meditation. Enhancing your yoga experience with mindfulness practice, compassion, and self-love will bring you lasting peace.

Chakras and Reiki

I am a big believer in the fact that energy imbalances in various parts of our body can cause physical pain and psychological disturbances. It is important to pay attention to such factors.

There are seven Chakras in our body aligned vertically, going from the base of the spine to the top of the crown of the forehead. Each chakra has its own significance. I have included a brief explanation of Chakras by Anodea Judith at the end of this chapter. Her book 'Wheels of Life: A user's Guide to the Chakra Systems' will be a great intro to Chakras.

There are tons of sources where you can find relevant information on Chakras. They are a world of their own. I want you to at least expose yourself to the concept of energies and Chakras.

I also recommend looking up Reiki and its benefits. Reiki is a healing art that has been practiced for centuries, which I have personally benefitted from. Hopefully, you can tap into the benefits of it as well.

First (Root) Chakra – Earth, grounding, home, work, finances, manifestation and being here. Located at the base of the spine, this chakra forms our foundation. It represents the element earth, and is therefore related to our survival instincts, and to our sense of grounding and connection to our bodies and the physical plane. Ideally this chakra brings us health, prosperity, security, and dynamic presence.

Second (Sacral) Chakra – Water, Emotional identity, oriented to self-gratification. The second chakra, located in the abdomen, lower back, and sexual organs, is related to the element water, and to emotions and sexuality. It connects us to others through feeling, desire, sensation, and movement. Ideally this chakra brings us fluidity and grace, depth of feeling, sexual fulfillment, and the ability to accept change.

Third (Solar Plexus) Chakra – Fire, energy, ego, power, will, risk, digestion, motivation and action. This chakra is known as the power chakra, located in the solar plexus. It rules our personal power, will, and autonomy, as well as our metabolism. When healthy, this chakra brings us energy, effectiveness, spontaneity, and non-dominating power.

Fourth (Heart) Chakra – Air, love, relationship, balance, breath, nurturing, and balance. This chakra is called the heart chakra and is the middle chakra in a system of seven. It is related to love and is the integrator of opposites in the psyche: mind and body, male and female, persona and shadow, ego and unity. A healthy fourth chakra allows us to love deeply, feel compassion, have a deep sense of peace and centeredness.

Fifth (Throat) Chakra – Sound, vibration, communication, self-expression, being heard. This is the chakra located in the throat and is thus related to communication and creativity. Here we experience the world symbolically through vibration, such as the vibration of sound representing language.

Sixth (Third Eye) Chakra – Light, vision, sight, perception, visualization, insight, dreaming. This chakra is known as the brow chakra or third eye center. It is related to the act of seeing, both physically and intuitively. As such it opens our psychic faculties and our understanding of archetypal levels. When healthy it allows us to see clearly, in effect, letting us "see the big picture."

Seventh (Crown) Chakra – Spiritual connection, beliefs, understanding, thought, and awareness. This is the crown chakra that relates to consciousness as pure awareness. It is our connection to the greater world beyond, to a timeless, space-less place of all-knowing. When developed, this chakra brings us knowledge, wisdom, understanding, spiritual connection, and bliss.

One or many of the Chakras can have imbalances that cause us to suffer in certain areas of life. Reiki healing can help with such imbalances.

Quiz Answers

Quiz 1: 1. C, 2. C, 3. B, 4. E
Quiz 2. 1. D, 2. C, 3. B, 4. B, 5. A
Quiz 3: 1. C., 2. B., 3. A

What of all the journal entries that I made?

First of all, thank you for doing the work. Journaling is a habit that I really hope you have started and will continue throughout this book.

If you started journaling, and have seen benefits from it, good for you! If you have not, you will see it in days to come, so please do not get discouraged by the lack of results.

I suggest you go back and review the answers to the Journal entries time and again. As you write more, and peel layers of the onion, you will find yourself easily resolving challenges that were major at some point in your past. This will be a very rewarding experience.

If you find yourself stuck in the same emotional state for a very long time, you will know that what you are doing is possibly not working. Then you can tinker with your strategy to make it work for you.

The idea behind releasing the negative patterns from your mind is to get you to act. Without action, change is not possible. By doing the exercises in your Journal, you already committed yourself to action. That was my motive behind the exercises throughout the book.

Recommendations

1. Louise Hay on "How to Love Yourself." By far the best talk on this topic.
   https://www.youtube.com/watch?v=oBOijSpYvcA
2. Mindfulness: An Eight Week Plan for Finding Peace in a Frantic World by Mark Williams and Danny Penman
   This is where I derived the mediation in the chapter "Mindfulness Practice" from.
3. The Law of Attraction Principles
   https://www.youtube.com/watch?v=7CkpMZr3PQk
4. Eliott Hulse is not just a trainer, but a philosopher. Great resource on life and strength
   https://www.youtube.com/user/elliottsaidwhat
5. Ralph Smart. He will give you a window to use to look into yourself
   https://www.youtube.com/user/Kemetprince1
6. Think and Grow Rich by Napoleon Hill
   This is a great book on how millionaires are created from scratch.
7. Tony Robbins on Massive Action, and Bonus Worksheet. Massive Action is a concept I credit to Tony
   https://www.tonyrobbins.com/career-business/how-to-make-a-massive-action-plan-map/
8. Kartika Nair, Synchro Shakti.
   https://www.youtube.com/user/SynchroShakti
   I have personally benefitted from her teachings. Bonus, she does Reggae music!

A word of caution: "Judge not by appearances." I suggest you read tons of material before deciding if anything is right or wrong for you.

If none of these recommendations resonate with you, that is OK. Go on to things that will serve you. In the end, this is about you, and what you consider worthy of experiencing. Experience your reality.

"Have a mind that is open to everything, but attached to nothing."   - Tilopa

IN THE END.

I thank you and congratulate you, both for staying with me until the end of this book and for the steps you have taken towards recreating your life. If this book helped you understand and internalize at least one concept, I am honored.

I also welcome you to an exciting new phase in your life, where you will tackle situations by falling back on the concepts I teach in this book. If you have done all the exercises I suggest in these pages, there is no doubt in my mind that you will be able to handle anything life throws your way.

If you are ever in a situation where you need to make a decision and do not know where to turn, ask yourself these three questions:

Is this decision Positive? Am I making this decision with Authenticity? Is this decision indicative of Self-Love?

The answer to these questions will help you make a sound decision.

I am sure that we will connect again. Look for me on the internet and send me a message. I would love to hear from you about your progress.

Good Luck!
Coach KP

28054906R00054

Made in the USA
Middletown, DE
19 December 2018